Making Your Own

WINE, BEER
& SOFT DRINKS

by PHYLLIS HOBSON

A Garden Way Guide
of HOMESTEAD RECIPES

GARDEN WAY PUBLISHING
CHARLOTTE, VERMONT, 05445

Library of Congress Catalog Card Number: 75-3494
ISBN 0-88266-063-2

Fifth Printing, December 1978

Designed by Frank Lieberman

PRINTED IN THE UNITED STATES

MAKING YOUR OWN

Long before bottled and canned beers and wines and soft drinks became available in almost every supermarket, Americans were making their own.

They made these beverages from many wholesome, homegrown ingredients with equipment they had on hand. With excess fruits from the orchard they made wines and bottled soft drinks.

They malted grains from the fields to brew homemade beer and ale. And using roots and barks from the forests they made that distinctly American beverage — root beer.

In this day of high prices and questionable quality, making your own home beverages can be a thrifty way to provide your family with healthful and delicious wines, beers and bottled soft drinks. It can also be an absorbing hobby or an interesting family project. Winemaking and beer brewing are skills that improve with practice, and producing your own fine beverages can be satisfying accomplishments.

It is possible to take shortcuts. You can buy canned malt extract or wort, which is an "instant beer" concentrate to which you need only add water and yeast and some form of sugar. Canned wort, from which ale or stout is made, is a malt extract to which hops water has been added.

You can buy mead mix and wine concentrates in every flavor from apple to zucchini, some natural and some not. And in certain areas of the country you will still find tiny bottles of root beer extract on the grocery shelves.

But if you're a homesteader you'll want to make your wine or beer or fruit drinks yourself from scratch. You'll want to use wholesome, homegrown ingredients and the equipment you have on hand.

Here's how:

MAKING WINES

YOU'LL NEED: A 4 to 5-gallon size crock will take care of most of our recipes, but if you're buying, get an 8 to 10 gallon crock. It doesn't cost much more and you'll probably grow into it. You can use it for lots of other things. The cheapest source of crocks is still the country auctions, although the price goes steadily upward even there. If necessary you can use clean plastic trash or garbage cans.

Gallon size glass jars — 2 or 3.

A small keg or barrel — not absolutely necessary, but if you happen to have one around it's simpler.

A funnel — for bottling and straining.

A siphon hose — a small rubber or plastic tube about 3 feet long will do.

A wooden spoon or paddle — buy or make a long-handled one.

An enamel or granite lined pot — the large, cheap hot water canners are great.

Straining cloths — several thicknesses of cheesecloth or old, soft muslin.

A masher — you can use a wooden or metal potato masher or a pastry blender to mash the fruit.

Fruit press or lard press — except for a few hard-to-squeeze fruits, this is a luxury item, but it will save a lot of time. We bought our heavy iron one for 50 cents at a farm auction.

Bottles — heavy soft drink bottles work just fine. They're available for the 3 to 5-cent deposit at most grocery stores. Do not use the throw-away, disposable bottles marked "Do not return."

Corks — to fit the bottles you're using. Almost any hardware store has a variety of sizes.

A capper — necessary for capping beers and soft drinks on which corks are not suitable. You can buy a used capper for $2-$3 or a new one for about $10. Caps come in boxes of 100 for about $1.

Large container — a wash boiler or laundry tub. You'll need a large container in which to mash the fruit or sprout the grain. See page 41 on How to Extract Juice From Fruits.

Most home wine recipes follow one basic procedure: fruit juice is mixed with sugar and yeast to start fermentation. It is then kept in a warm (65 to 75 degrees) place two or three weeks in an open crock or cask loosely covered with a cloth to keep out insects and dust.

At this stage, the wine will grow daily, sometimes overflowing the crock. After two or three weeks of active fermentation, (the length of time will depend on the temperature, the amount of sugar added as well as that already in the fruit, the amount of yeast and the season) visible fermentation will slow down and the liquid level fall in the crock or cask.

Now the scum is skimmed or flowed off the top and the liquid is siphoned or strained into another crock or into one-gallon jars or jugs. (Restaurant mayonnaise or pickle jars are good for this.) In siphoning, be careful the hose does not touch the sediment in the bottom of the crock. To strain off the liquid, carefully dip out the top 3/4 of the liquid. The bottom 1/4 may be strained into a separate jar or crock.

At this point, it's a good idea to taste the wine for sweetness. If you like a sweet wine, you may want to add more sugar. Just dissolve the sugar in hot water and cool before adding.

Now loosely cover the jars or crock and let the green wine stand one or two weeks. If you look closely, you can still see small fermenting bubbles.

As soon as the wine stops working, siphon the wine into bottles and cork loosely. Once again, avoid the sediment in the bottom of the crock or jar. Stand the bottles upright for one week, then tighten corks and lay down on racks (or a shelf tilted at an angle) so that the corks are kept wet by the liquid.

Leave the wine there, cool, quiet and undisturbed, for at least six months. A year or two is better. It's worth the wait.

RACKING

After the wine has been bottled a few weeks or a few months, you'll notice a sediment has settled to the bottom, or, when the bottle is lying down, on the side of the bottle. If you like your wine as clear as clear can be, you can "rack" it. Just pour the wine into another bottle, carefully, so as not to disturb the sediment, and discard the sediment. You'll have to add more wine in order to bring the liquid up to the cork, so it's best to rack several bottles at once and use up one bottle to refill the rest. Some winemakers rack their wine every few months to keep it as clear as possible.

INGREDIENTS   Fruit juice, sugar, a little time in a warm spot.

That's all. You don't even need the sugar if the fruit is sweet enough and you like your wine dry. But all of our recipes call for sugar for better fermentation. Most of them also call for yeast, but wine can be made without it. We recommend it for more predictable fermentation.

You can use almost any kind of fruit for wine, but be fussy about the quality. If it isn't good fruit, it won't be good wine. The fruit should be ripe and juicy. And it must not have been sprayed or treated with preservatives or the wine will sour without fermenting.

The juices of any fruits — and some vegetables — can be used to make a variety of wines, either alone or in combinations. The best wine is made from perfectly ripe fruit. But you needn't fuss with preparing the fruit. Just wash it and toss it in — rind, peeling, seeds and all. The excess will be strained off later and it won't hurt a thing. Few fruits except pineapple need to be peeled.

WINE RECIPES

(Instructions for extracting juices are on page 41)

APPLE WINE   2½ gallons apple juice
2 pounds sugar
2 packages dry yeast

Heat juice enough to dissolve sugar, then cool to lukewarm and add yeast. Pour into crock. Ferment two to three weeks, skimming every day. When bubbling stops,

strain into glass jars or a clean crock. Let rest, loosely covered, two weeks. Bottle and cork loosely. Check in a week or two to make sure all bubbling has stopped. When it has, cork tightly and lay bottles down. Age 1 year..

9

OR:

Apple cider may be substituted for the apple juice in the above recipe if no preservatives have been used in the cider.

OR:

16 pounds chopped apples (include cores)
2 gallons boiling water
4 pounds sugar
2 packages yeast

Pour boiling water over chopped apples in crock. Add sugar and stir to dissolve. Let stand 3 or 4 days, stirring occasionally, then strain and return juice to crock. Add yeast and let ferment two to three weeks. Proceed as in first recipe.

OR:

Use recipe above, adding two sliced lemons and two sliced oranges to the chopped apples.

OR:

To make a barrel or keg of apple wine, fill a keg or barrel with apple juice, fresh from the fruit press. When half full, add 1½ pounds of brown sugar for every gallon of juice. Mix well, then continue filling the container. Put the cask in a cool place, leaving the bung out 48 hours, then putting it in loosely with a small air vent until fermentation ceases. Then bung up tight and set stand 1 year. The longer it stands, the better.

APRICOT WINE

2 gallons water
4 pounds sugar
24 pounds ripe apricots
2 packages yeast

Mash apricots in small amount of water. Add sugar to rest of water and bring to a boil, stirring, until sugar is dissolved. Add apricots and boil about one hour. Strain into crock and cool to lukewarm. Add dissolved yeast. Cover with a cloth and let ferment two to three weeks. Siphon into another crock, let rest one week, then bottle.

OR:

2½ gallons water
3 pounds rice
2 lemons
3 pounds dried apricots
5 pounds sugar
2 packages yeast

Cook rice in boiling water. Drain off cooked rice, saving water. Rice may be eaten. Add apricots to rice water and let soak one hour, then simmer one hour. Mash cooked apricots and drain juice into crock. Dissolve sugar in juice, stirring constantly. Cool to lukewarm and add yeast and juice of two lemons. Cover with cheesecloth and let ferment two to three weeks. Siphon into another crock or gallon glass jars and let rest one week. Then bottle and cork.

BANANA WINE

2 gallons water
10 bananas
2 oranges
1 lemon
5 pounds sugar
3 cakes yeast

Mash bananas in small amount of water, then add remaining water. Slice oranges and lemon thinly, then add. Add sugar, stirring constantly to dissolve. Over low heat, gently simmer ½ hour. Strain into crock and cool to lukewarm, then add yeast dissolved in ½ cup warm water. Stir thoroughly to mix. Let ferment two weeks, or until it stops bubbling actively. Siphon to glass gallon jars, cork loosely and let rest one week to finish fermenting. Siphon into bottles, filling almost to the top and corking loosely. Stand bottles upright in a cool place one week, then tighten corks and lay on sides. Age 6 to 8 months. This wine does not keep well.

BLACKBERRY WINE

To every gallon of bruised fruit, add ½ gallon cold water. Let stand 24 hours, then strain. To every gallon of juice, add 3 pounds sugar. Fill a cask or crock and let it remain without moving or shaking until it has fermented. Draw off wine and bottle.

OR:

Half fill a large crock with ripe blackberries. Cover with water, mash the berries and let stand overnight. In the morning, strain through a thick cloth and add 3 pounds sugar to each gallon of juice. Let it ferment two to three weeks, stirring and skimming each day. Siphon off wine and bottle.

OR:

Mash one bushel of very ripe berries and pour one bucket boiling water over them. Cover and let stand 24 hours. Strain through a cloth and to every 3 quarts juice add 2 quarts cold water and 5 pounds brown sugar. Let ferment one week, then add 1 envelope gelatin softened in ¼ cup cold water, then dissolved in 1 cup hot water. Let ferment two weeks more, then cork tightly in a cask and leave undisturbed six months. Bottle and seal.

OR:

Fill a large stone jar with ripe blackberries and cover with water. Tie a cloth over the jar and let stand 3 or 4 days to ferment. Then mash and press fruit through a cloth. To every gallon of juice add 3 pounds brown sugar. Return mixture to the crock and cover closely. Skim it every morning for more than a week until it clears from the second fermentation. When the liquid is clear, pour it carefully, to prevent disturbing the sediment, into a demijohn. Cork tightly; set in a cool place. In two months it is ready for use.

OR:

To every gallon of berries, add one quart boiling water. Let stand 12 hours. Strain. To every gallon of juice, add 2 pounds sugar, stirring until sugar is well dissolved. Pour into jugs, filling to the brim so as the juice ferments the scum will flow off. Each morning refill the jugs with juice from a bottle kept for this purpose. Repeat for five days or until fermenting stops, then close jugs loosely. After another five days, cork tightly and let stand in a cool place for four months. At the end of that time, siphon off the clear liquid carefully, bottle and seal.

BLUEBERRY WINE

8 quarts blueberries
2 gallons water
5 pounds sugar
2 packages dry yeast

13

Mash blueberries to release juice. Add water and sugar and simmer, stirring occasionally, for 30 minutes. Strain into crock and cool to lukewarm. Add yeast dissolved in small amount of juice and let ferment two to three weeks before bottling.

CHERRY WINE

Press the juice from ripe cherries, being careful not to mash stones. To every gallon of juice, add 2 pounds sugar. Dissolve and allow to ferment in a crock or keg until fermentation ceases.

In a keg, bung tightly and let set 3 or 4 months, then bottle. If fermented in a crock, bottle and cork loosely for 2 to 3 weeks, then cork tightly. It is ready to drink in 6 months.

OR:

10 pounds cherries
2 gallons water
3 pounds sugar
2 cakes yeast

Mash cherries and cover with cold water. Let stand two days, stirring occasionally. Strain into crock. Add yeast dissolved in warm water. Mix thoroughly and cover with a cloth. Let ferment two weeks, skimming occasionally. Siphon into glass jars or a clean crock and let rest one week. Bottle and cork loosely. Stand upright on a shelf in cool, dark place. After two weeks, tighten corks and lay bottles so corks are kept moist and wine can "breathe." Age two years before using.

14

OR:

10 pounds ripe cherries
2 gallons water
6 to 8 pounds sugar
2 cakes yeast

Mash cherries in large enamel pan. Add sugar and water and stir to dissolve. Bring to a boil over low heat, stirring occasionally, and simmer 15 to 20 minutes. Turn off heat and let it cool to warm. Strain into crock and add dissolved yeast. Let ferment two weeks then strain and bottle.

OR:

To every gallon of cherries, add 1 quart boiling water. Bruise fruit and let stand in crock 24 hours, stirring occasionally. Strain off liquid and add 2 pounds sugar to every gallon juice. Ferment two to three weeks, or until bubbling stops, then strain and bottle.

OR:

1 pound raisins
1 pound dried cherries
12 prunes
2 pounds brown sugar
1 gallon water
1 package yeast

Grind fruits through food chopper. Add brown sugar and cover with boiling water. Let soak overnight. In the morning, set over low heat and simmer for 1 hour. Cool, then strain into crock and add dissolved yeast. Ferment two to three weeks. Strain and bottle.

CIDER WINE

To 1 gallon sweet cider, add 3 pounds sugar. Pour into a small cask and let ferment 15 days, putting the cork in a little tighter each day. Let stand 3 months, then bottle and seal.

CLOVER WINE

6 to 8 quarts clover blossoms
2 gallons boiling water
5 to 6 pounds sugar
4 lemons
4 oranges
3 cakes yeast

Remove all stems from blossoms and place in an enamel pan. Pour boiling water over blossoms and add sugar, sliced lemon and sliced oranges. Simmer 30 minutes. Turn off heat and cool to lukewarm. Strain into crock and add crumbled yeast. Stir well. Ferment two weeks. When liquid stops bubbling, siphon into glass jars or a clean crock and let rest, covered loosely, for one week. Bottle as usual.

CRANBERRY WINE

8 quarts cranberries
2 gallons water
6 pounds sugar
3 packages yeast

Pour water over cranberries and sugar in enamel pan. Simmer over low heat until berries burst. Stir well and turn off heat. Cool to warm, then strain juice into crock. When liquid is lukewarm, add yeast and set in a warm place to ferment. This wine is especially colorful when it clears.

CURRANT WINE

8 quarts currants
2 gallons water
5 pounds sugar

Follow directions for Cranberry Wine. Yeast should not be necessary. Fermentation should begin within 3 days.

OR:

Strip 4 gallons ripe currants from the stalks into a stone crock. Mash with a mallet. Let stand 24 hours, then strain through a jelly bag. Clean the crock and pour the juice back. Meanwhile, boil 5 pounds sugar in 2½ gallons water, skimming it well. When the scum ceases to rise, mix the syrup with the currant juice. Let stand 3 weeks, then transfer to another crock, taking care not to disturb the sediment. If the wine is not clear, refine it by taking out 1 quart and mixing with it 2 egg whites, stiffly beaten, and ½ ounce cream of tartar. Mix well, then pour back into the crock. Let stand 10 days more, then bottle and cork. Place the bottles in sawdust, laying them on their sides. May be used after 3 months, but it improves with age.

DANDELION WINE

8 quarts dandelion flowers
2 gallons water
3 oranges
3 lemons
5 pounds sugar
2 cakes yeast

Carefully remove all traces of stems. Place flowers in crock; add sugar, sliced oranges and lemons and pour boiling water over all. Let set two days, stirring occasionally. On the third day, strain into another crock and add yeast. Let ferment two weeks in a warm place.

ELDERBERRY WINE

2 gallons elderberries
2 gallons water
6 pounds sugar
2 cakes yeast

Bruise fruit. Add sugar and boiling water and stir to dissolve sugar. Let set in crock three days. If fermentation has not started in that time, strain off juice and add yeast to it. Mix well. Let ferment two weeks, then strain and bottle.

OR:

Put the elderberries in a stone crock set in a pan of hot water. Crush the berries and place over low heat until juice begins to simmer. Strain juice and to every quart of juice add 1 pound of sugar and 2 quarts of soft water. Boil and skim this mixture until scum ceases to rise. To every 4 gallons of this liquid, add 1 pint of brandy. Pour into a keg and let stand, loosely bunged, for 4 or 5 days. When it has ceased to ferment, bung tightly, plastering the bung with clay. After 6 months, draw off a little. If it is not yet clear and bright, refine it by adding the whites and shells of 3 eggs, beaten to a stiff froth and stirred into a quart of the wine. Return this to the keg and let stand a week longer. Bottle and cork tightly.

ELDER BLOSSOM WINE

1 quart elderberry blossoms
6 pounds sugar
2 cakes yeast
2 gallons water
3 pounds raisins
2 lemons

The blossoms should be picked carefully from the stems and the quart measure packed full. Dissolve sugar in

18

water over heat and let boil five minutes without stirring. Skim and add the blossoms. As soon as the blossoms are stirred in, remove from the heat source and cool. When lukewarm, add the dissolved yeast and sliced lemons. Let stand in crock six days, stirring thoroughly three times a day. The blossoms must be stirred from the bottom of the jar each time. On the seventh day, strain through a cloth and add the raisins. Put in glass jars and cover tightly. Do not bottle and cork until January.

GRAPE WINE

Pick grapes from the bunch, mash thoroughly and let stand two days. Squeeze out juice (with a wine press, if you have one) and to every gallon of juice add 3 pounds sugar. Strain into a cask, cover the bung hole with a piece of muslin so the gas can escape and insects cannot get in. Keep in a warm place until cold weather, then bung up tightly.

OR:

Press the grapes and when the juice settles add 2 pounds sugar to four quarts juice. Let stand 24 hours, drain and put in cask. Do not stop bung tightly until fermentation is over.

OR:

Put 20 pounds of ripe, freshly-picked grapes into a crock and pour 6 quarts of boiling water over them. Cool, then squeeze grapes by hand or with a soft mallet to break skins.

Stir well, cover the crock with a cloth and let stand 3 days. Strain off juice, discard pomace and clean the crock. Pour the juice back in and add 10 pounds sugar and let set 1 week, covered, in a warm place. Then skim, strain and bottle. Stopper the bottles loosely with cotton and stand upright on shelves at 70 degrees. When fermenting has ceased, pour the clear liquid into clean bottles, discarding the sediment in the bottom of the bottles. Cap or tightly cork the bottles and lay on their sides in a cool place (40 to 50 degrees).

CATAWBA GRAPE WINE

To every gallon of grape juice add one quart cold water and 3 pounds sugar. Pour into jug and let it ferment, uncorked, 14 days, then cork loosely. Add 1 envelope unflavored gelatin softened in ¼ cup cold water, then dissolved in ½ cup hot water. Let rest another 14 days, then tighten cork and let it remain undisturbed six months. Strain, bottle and cork.

FOX GRAPE WINE

To every bushel of fox grapes, pour over 4 gallons boiling water. Mash fruit and let stand 24 hours. Strain into crock or cask and add 2 pounds sugar for every gallon of juice. Ferment two weeks.

WILD BLACK GRAPE WINE

Mash grapes and just cover with boiling water. Let set 24 hours and strain. For every gallon of juice, add 3 pounds sugar. Ferment 2 to 3 weeks before bottling. Must be aged at least 1 year.

GRAPEFRUIT WINE

14 grapefruit
3 gallons water
10 pounds sugar

Squeeze the juice from the grapefruit and add the sugar which has been dissolved in the water. Let ferment two to three weeks, or until bubbles have stopped. Siphon off clear liquid into glass jars and let rest one week. Bottle as usual.

OR:

1 pound barley
2 gallons water
10 grapefruit
10 pounds sugar

Cook barley in water 1 hour. Strain, reserving water. Squeeze juice from fruit and add to water in which sugar has been dissolved. Pour into crock and set to ferment. Bottle as in first recipe.

GOOSEBERRY WINE

To every gallon of gooseberries add 3 pints boiling water. Let stand two days, then mash and squeeze out the juice. To every gallon of juice add 3 pounds sugar. Let ferment 2 to 3 weeks, then siphon off clear liquid into jars and let rest one weeks. Bottle and cork.

LEMON WINE

20 lemons
2 gallons water
8 pounds sugar
1 pound raisins
2 packages yeast

21

Slice lemons in thin slices. Add sugar and raisins and pour the boiling water over them. Let stand three days, then add yeast dissolved in warm water. Let ferment two to three weeks, then siphon off into jars or another crock. Let set one week, then bottle and cork.

ORANGE WINE

4 quarts orange juice
1 gallon water
4 pounds sugar
grated rind of 4 oranges
2 cakes yeast

Dissolve sugar in 1 quart boiling water, then add to juice, grated rind and remaining water in crock. Add yeast and ferment two weeks. Strain and bottle.

OR:

25 oranges
1½ gallons water
4 pounds sugar
2 cakes yeast

Grind oranges, including rind, in food chopper and combine with sugar which has been dissolved in hot water. Mix all ingredients, including yeast, in a warm crock. Set in a warm, dark place and let ferment two to three weeks. Strain or siphon clear liquid off the top and bottle. This wine can be used in six weeks.

PASSOVER WINE

Put two pounds raisins, (chop them a little) in a stone crock. Pour 1 gallon boiling water over them and add one-half lemon, sliced thin. Cover lightly and let stand two or three days, stirring every day. Strain twice, bottle and set in a cool place.

22

PEACH WINE

12 to 15 pounds peaches
6 to 8 pounds sugar
2 gallons water
2 lemons
2 oranges
3 packages yeast

Mash peaches and combine with sugar, water, lemons and oranges in an enamel pan. Simmer 1 hour, cool and strain into a crock. When cooled to lukewarm, add yeast and stir well. Ferment two to three weeks, or until bubbling stops. Strain into a clean crock and let rest one week. Then bottle and cork.

OR:

40 to 50 peaches
4 pounds sugar
2½ gallons water
2 lemons
2 oranges
3 cakes yeast

Mash peaches in crock. Add sliced lemons and oranges, sugar and boiling water. Let stand 3 days. If fermentation has not started in that time, add yeast. Ferment two to three weeks, then strain and bottle, corking loosely. After 1 week tighten corks.

PEAR WINE

10 to 15 pounds ripe pears
2 gallons water
3 to 4 pounds sugar
4 lemons
2 oranges
1 pound raisins
3 cakes yeast

Mash pears and add sliced oranges and lemons. Simmer in water ½ hour, then cool and strain. Add dissolved yeast and pour into crock to ferment. When all bubbling has stopped, skim and siphon into glass jars. Let settle one week, then bottle and cork.

PINEAPPLE WINE

8 quarts chopped pineapple
2 gallons water
6 pounds sugar
3 cakes yeast

Combine and simmer pineapple, sugar and water over low heat for 1 hour. Cool, mash into a pulp and strain into a crock. When mixture is lukewarm, add yeast which has been dissolved in ½ cup warm water. Let ferment two to three weeks. Skim and siphon into gallon jars. After 1 week, bottle and cork.

OR:

If you have a fruit press, you may press out the juice and make this uncooked wine:
2 gallons boiling water
8 to 10 pineapples
6 pounds sugar
2 lemons
3 packages yeast

24

Put pineapples and lemons through a fruit press. To juice obtained, add sugar and water in a crock. Add dissolved yeast and let ferment two to three weeks. Then let rest one week, bottle and cork.

PLUM WINE

2 gallons water
6 to 8 pounds sugar
20 pounds plums
3 cakes yeast

The amount of sugar depends on the tartness of the plums and how sweet you like your wine. Any kind or any mixture of plums may be used. Red plums make the brightest wine.

Mash plums in small amount of water in an enamel pan. Add sugar and remaining water and simmer over heat for one to two hours. Strain juice into a crock. When cooled to lukewarm, add yeast dissolved in ½ cup warm water. Let ferment about two weeks, or until it stops bubbling. Let rest one week, then bottle and cork. Let age one year or more for best flavor.

OR:

15 pounds plums
2 lemons
2 oranges
½ ounce ginger root
10 cloves
3 peppercorns
2 cinnamon sticks
2 gallons water
6 pounds brown sugar
3 cakes yeast

25

Tie spices in a spice bag and tuck under the fruit in the bottom of the crock. Add boiling water and let stand one week, stirring two or three times a day. On the eighth day, strain, add sugar and dissolved yeast. Ferment two or three weeks. This is a rich, heavy wine.

PORT WINE To 2 bushels of wild grapes, add 25 pounds sugar and enough water to cover. Mash grapes, then put into a 55-gallon barrel and fill with rain water. Let this stand in the sun for a few weeks. Then place in the cellar until spring. Rack off and bottle.

PRUNE WINE

5 pounds prunes
2 gallons water
6 pounds sugar
2 packages yeast

Pour boiling water over prunes and sugar. Stir to dissolve sugar, then let soak overnight. In the morning, simmer slowly two hours, then mash prunes with potato masher or pastry cutter. Let set until lukewarm, then strain juice into warm crock. Add yeast dissolved in small amount of juice, cover crock with a cloth and let ferment until it stops bubbling, then siphon off into a clean crock or glass jars. Let rest 1 week, then bottle and cork.

RAISIN WINE

6 pounds raisins
3 lemons
2 gallons water
6 pounds sugar
2 packages yeast

Follow directions for Prune Wine.

OR:

Seed and chop 2 pounds raisins. Add a thinly sliced lemon, 2 cups sugar and 2 gallons boiling water. Pour into a stone jar and stir each day for 6 to 8 days. When it has ceased working, strain, bottle and cork, then set the bottles in a cool place. The wine is at its best after two months.

OR:

Into a stone crock put 1 pound of sugar, 2 pounds of chopped seeded raisins, the juice of 1 lemon and the grated peel. After mixing well pour in 2 gallons of boiling water. Cover and set in warm, draft-free place. Stir every day for a week, then strain and bottle. It will be ready in 10 days.

RHUBARB WINE

8 pounds rhubarb
grated rind of 4 lemons
8 quarts boiling water
6 pounds sugar

Cut up rhubarb and add lemon rind and water. Let stand 3 days in a covered crock. Strain and discard rhubarb, then add sugar to liquid and pour back into crock. Cover loosely and let stand 2 weeks. Cover with a tight-fitting lid. At the end of 1 month it will be ready to bottle.

OR:

Wash and cut rhubarb into 1-inch lengths. Cook in small amounts over very low heat, adding only 1 cup water for a kettle of fruit. In 20 to 30 minutes, the rhubarb will be cooked, leaving juice and a stringy pulp. Strain the juice into a small keg, adding 3½ pounds of sugar for each gallon

27

of juice. Leave the keg open as the wine ferments, adding sweetened water every few days to fill. When clear, bung it down and let stand in an undisturbed spot until spring. Then bottle and cork.

OR:
10 pounds rhubarb
2 gallons water
6 to 8 pounds sugar
2 packages yeast

Cook rhubarb and sugar in water, stirring to dissolve sugar and reduce rhubarb to a pulp. Simmer about ½ hour, then cool to lukewarm and strain into crock. Dissolve yeast in ½ cup juice and add, stirring to mix thoroughly. Let ferment two to three weeks. Siphon into clean crock or glass jars and let rest one week. Age at least one year.

ROSE HIPS WINE

2 quarts rose hips
2 gallons water
6 pounds sugar
2 packages yeast

Crush rose hips in hot water in crock. Add sugar and cool to lukewarm, then add yeast and stir well. Let ferment two weeks, then strain and bottle. This wine is very high in Vitamin C and can be used within 6 months.

SCUPPERNONG WINE

Gather ripe but firm grapes. Wash and to every gallon of grapes, add one quart boiling water. Let stand 24 hours. Strain off juice and to every gallon of juice add 2½ pounds sugar. Mix thoroughly and let stand again 24 hours. Skim, strain and pour into jugs. Cover each jug with thin muslin cloth. Let mixture stand six to eight weeks, adding juice from time to time to flow off the scum and replacing the cloth to keep out dust and insects. When fermenting stops, strain through a flannel bag, bottle and cork. Wine will be ready a few weeks after bottling.

STRAWBERRY WINE

To each gallon of mashed strawberries add ½ gallon boiling water. Let stand 24 hours, then strain and add 3 pounds sugar to each gallon juice. Let stand 36 hours, and skim. Put in cask, saving some juice to add as it overflows. Fill each morning. Bottle and cork when fermentation stops.

OR:

Mash and strain 3 quarts of strawberries. To the juice, add 1 pound of sugar and 1 quart of water. Stir well, then set aside in a crock to ferment. When it stops fermenting, bottle and cork tightly.

TOMATO WINE

2 gallons tomato juice
4 pounds sugar
2 packages yeast

Dissolve sugar in small amount of hot juice. Mix with remaining juice in crock and let stand overnight. In the morning, add yeast and stir until dissolved. Ferment two to three weeks, then skim and siphon off to glass jars. Let rest one week, bottle and cork loosely. After one week, tighten corks and lay bottles on rack to mature. Good after one year.

OR

Mash 1 bushel tomatoes in a granite or enamel pan and heat just to boiling, stirring occasionally. Strain through a sieve into an 8-gallon crock and add 2 pounds of sugar for each gallon of juice. Cover and let set overnight. In the morning stir in 3 yeast cakes which have been dissolved in warm water. Ferment as above.

MAKING MEADS,
BRANDIES & CORDIALS

Mead is a sweet wine made of honey and water, sometimes spiced with cloves and cinnamon. Simple mead is probably one of the first wines produced by man. The best mead is made from dark wood honeys.

SIMPLE MEAD   Dissolve 5 pounds of dark honey in 1 gallon of lukewarm water. Stir to dissolve, then add 1 teaspoon dry yeast and stir again. Pour into a crock and cover with cheesecloth. Let ferment about 3 weeks, or until activity stops. Strain and bottle, corking lightly for 1 week, then tightening corks. Store in a cool place for 3 months before drinking.

APPLE MEAD   Dissolve 1 gallon of honey in 1 gallon of fresh sweet cider. Pour into a five-gallon crock and set in a warm, (70 to 80-degree) draft-free place. Cover with a cloth and let set 2 to 3 weeks, or until all fermentation stops. Bottle, cork loosely and stand upright in a cool place. When there are no signs of tiny bubbles, tighten corks and lay bottles on their sides. The wine will be ready to drink in 6 months, but will improve with age.

CURRANT MEAD   To 2 gallons boiling water, add 9 pounds honey, 2 pounds chopped seedless raisins and 1½ gallons red currant juice. Stir well to dissolve honey, then pour into a five-gallon crock and cool to lukewarm. Add 1 cup homemade liquid yeast (or 1 yeast cake dissolved in 1 cup water) and stir well. Cover and let stand in a warm (70-80 degree) place

THAT'S BRAGGET

'TAIN'T, IT'S MEAD

2 to 3 weeks. When active fermenting stops, bottle, corking loosely, and stand bottles upright on a shelf in a cool storage room. Check every week to see if tiny bubbles have ceased, then cork tightly and lay bottles on their sides. It is ready to drink in 6 to 9 months.

OLD ENGLISH BRAGGET

Also called mead, metheglin and hydromel, this very ancient beverage may be made by combining and mixing thoroughly, 28 pounds of honey with 8½ gallons boiling water in a crock. Then, in a pan, add the peel of 3 lemons, 1 ounce of dried ginger root, bruised, 2 teaspoons whole cloves and a small bunch of rosemary to ½ gallon of water. Boil 10 minutes, then strain immediately into the honey mixture. Stir well and set aside until cold. Then add 1 cup liquid yeast (or 1 yeast cake dissolved in warm water) and mix well. Pour into a wooden cask or keg and allow it to ferment, then bung tightly. Leave undisturbed 1 year, then bottle and cork and keep 6 months before drinking.

BLACKBERRY BRANDY

To every half gallon of blackberry juice, add 1½ pounds sugar, ½ teaspoon ground cinnamon, ½ teaspoon grated nutmeg, ¼ teaspoon ground cloves and 1 teaspoon allspice. Simmer over low heat a few minutes, then strain through three thicknesses of cheesecloth. Cool, then add 1 pint of brandy.

CHERRY BRANDY

Gently mash 36 pounds ripe cherries without breaking the stones. Squeeze with the hands and pour 1½ gallons of brandy over them. Let infuse 24 hours, then strain through jelly bag, pressing the bag as long as the juice will run. Sweeten to taste with sugar (1 to 1½ pounds to every gallon) and let stand in covered crock one month. Bottle and cork.

MIXED CHERRY BRANDY Use recipe above, but for every gallon of brandy use 4 pounds of red cherries, 2 pounds of black cherries, 1 quart of raspberries, a few whole cloves, a stick of cinnamon and the grated peel of one orange.

MULLED WINE To a pint of water add 1 beaten nutmeg, 2 broken sticks of cinnamon, and 1 tablespoon whole cloves. Boil until the water is reduced to one-half, then strain the liquid into a quart of wine. Bring the wine just to a boil, then remove immediately from the heat. Add sugar to taste and serve hot.

OR:

Boil 16 cloves in 2 cups of water for 10 minutes. Meanwhile, beat 3 egg yolks well with 2 tablespoons sugar. Strain cloves from water and to the water add 2 cups wine and 1 tablespoon lemon juice. Heat to boiling while you beat the egg whites stiffly. Beat liquid into egg yolk mixture, then fold in egg whites. Serve hot.

MINT JULEP Finely chop 1 bunch mint leaves. Add 2 cups ice water and let stand overnight. Heat 2 cups of sugar in 4 cups of water until sugar dissolves, then chill. To this add the juice of 2 lemons and the strained mint water. Serve with crushed ice.

OR:
Put 3 sprigs mint with ½ teaspoon orange bitters in a glass. Add 1 sherry glass of vermouth and ½ cup whiskey. Shake well. Add ½ cup crushed ice, stirring to crush the mint. Add 2 slices of orange, 2 or 3 strawberries and a few more sprigs of mint. Serve in frosted glasses.

BLACKBERRY CORDIAL

To ½ bushel of blackberries, well mashed, add 2 teaspoons of ground allspice, 1 teaspoon ground cinnamon and 2 teaspoons ground cloves. Simmer over low heat to extract juice, then strain through three thicknesses of cheesecloth. To each pint of juice add 1 pound of sugar. Heat to dissolve sugar. Remove from stove and while cooling, add 1 quart of brandy.

RED CURRANT CORDIAL

To 2 quarts of red currants add 1 quart whiskey. Let stand 24 hours, then mash fruit and strain through cheesecloth. To each 2 quarts liquor add 1 pound sugar. Add 4 ounces dried, bruised ginger root which has been boiled 20 minutes in 1 pint of water. Let set overnight, then strain, bottle and cork. It will be ready to use in 1 month.

CHERRY BOUNCE

Mix 6 pounds of ripe red cherries with 6 pounds ripe black cherries. Put them in a wooden tub and with pestle or mallet mash them to crack all the stones. Mix with 3 pounds sugar and put them in a large stone jar. Pour 2 gallons whisky over the cherries. Cover tightly and let stand 3 months, shaking every day for the first month. At the end of 3 months, strain off the liquor and bottle it. It improves with age.

MAKING GRAIN BEERS

Beers are low (or non-) alcoholic beverages which depend on the slow action of a small amount of yeast or hops for their effervescence. They usually are made of malted grains. Occasionally the flavor comes from spices.

Grain beer, which has an alcoholic content of three to seven per cent, is made by malting grain (usually barley), then adding hot water to make a mash, and holding it at that temperature several hours to extract the flavor.

To this malt-flavored water is added sugar and yeast (or hops water) and the liquid is allowed to ferment before being bottled.

The length of time for "working" given in each recipe is only approximate, and will give the lowest alcoholic percentage. For maximum alcohol content the beer batch should be allowed to ferment until the brew almost — but not quite — stops working. These recipes come largely from old family cookbooks. The beermaking was intended for family use and back then was a health drink.

Most light beers are made from malted barley. The heavier flavor of ale and stout is created by adding corn or oats or bran during the mashing period.

HOME BREWED GRAIN BEERS

To make malt extract:
Wash ½ bushel of barley, then pour it into a laundry tub and cover with warm water and let set covered for three days, keeping it at room floor temperature (about 60 degrees).

At the end of three days drain. Discard water, but keep the barley wet and let set until the seeds germinate, a week to 10 days, stirring carefully 3 to 4 times a day.

When the seeds have sprouted, dry on trays in the sun, then roast them in an oven until golden brown. Oven temperatures should be 150 to 180 degrees for pale beers, 185 to 225 for ale and stout.

You now have malted grain from which the beer mash is made.

To mash the malted grain:
Grind the grain or crush with a rolling pin or wooden masher in the tub. Cover with hot (170 to 180 degree) water

and set it in the hot sun or over low heat to hold that temperature for 3 to 6 hours. Then strain the liquid into a crock and discard the spent grain.

SUBSTITUTIONS

The following substitutions can be made in any of the home-made beer recipes:

One pound dried malt extract for 3 pounds malt syrup or ½ bushel of grain, malted.

One 7-gram package of beer yeast for 1 cake of yeast, 1 package dried yeast or 1 cup homemade liquid yeast.

One 2½ ounce package of hops pellets for ¼ pound dried hops.

ENGLISH BEER

Malt ½ bushel of barley. When it is dry, coarsely grind and put into a clean metal laundry tub. Over the malt pour 3½ gallons hot (170 to 175 degrees) water. Let stand 3 hours. Strain off the water, pouring liquid into a large crock or keg.

Then pour 6 gallons hot (180 to 185 degrees) water over the same malt. Stir well and let stand another 3 hours. Now strain the liquid into the crock with the other liquid and discard the spent grain.

Pour the liquid into a tub or boiler and add 6 pounds raw sugar and ¼ pound hops. Simmer 2 hours over medium heat, then strain back into the crock and let cool to 80 degrees. Add 1 cup liquid yeast (or 1 yeast cake dissolved in 1 cup warm water). Stir well and cover with a cloth.

Let work for 24 hours. Bottle and cap and let set undisturbed for two weeks. (Or use a wooden keg, bunging it tight.) The beer is ready for use in 2 weeks, but will keep well, improving with age, for up to one year.

BRAN BEER

For 18 gallons of beer, pour 10 gallons hot water over 1 bushel of malted bran. Stir well and let stand 3 hours. Then strain off the wort into a crock and pour on another 10 gallons of hot water and let stand again 3 hours. Add the liquid to the crock and discard the spent bran.

Take out 4 gallons of the crock liquid and add ¼ pound of hops to it. Boil with 4 pounds of molasses for about 1 hour over low heat. Add this back to crock liquid and let cool to lukewarm. Stir in 1 cup liquid homemade yeast (or 1 yeast cake dissolved in 1 cup warm water.) Stir well and cover with a cloth. Let set 24 hours, then bottle and cap. Leave undisturbed 2 weeks. Will keep up to 1 year.

HOME BREWED ALE BY THE BARREL

For a barrel (36 gallons) of ale, you'll need:
    4 bushels of malted grain
    6 pounds of hops
    2½ quarts homemade liquid yeast (or 10 cakes yeast dissolved in 2 quarts lukewarm water)

Grind the dried malt into a metal tub and over it pour 20 gallons of water heated to 170 degrees. Stir well, cover and let stand 3 hours, keeping as warm as possible. Strain off this liquid and add it to the hops in a metal wash boiler.

Now add another 30 gallons of 170 degree water to the malt in the mash tub and mix well. Let stand 2 hours and strain it off, reserving liquid.

Meanwhile, boil the wort from the first mash with the hops for 2 hours over low heat. Cool to 80 degrees and strain. Mix with the wort from the second mash and pour into a large fermenting tub. Mix with the yeast and cover. Let work 24 to 30 hours. Then pour it into the barrel and leave the bung open another 24 hours. Then bung tightly and store in a cool place. It will be ready in 2 weeks. It may be used right from the barrel without bottled.

HOPS BEER Boil a handful of hops in 1 quart of water. Strain into a crock, then add 1 teaspoon ground ginger, 1 pint molasses, 3 gallons of lukewarm water and 1 cup liquid homemade yeast (or 1 cake yeast dissolved in 1 cup warm water). Cover and let stand 24 hours. Then skim, bottle and cap.

CORN BEER (without yeast) To an 8-gallon wooden keg, add 5 gallons cold water, 1 quart cracked, dried corn and 2 quarts molasses. Shake well and let ferment 3 days before using. Keep bung tight.

MIXED GRAIN BEER In 15 gallons of water mix ½ gallon malted barley, ½ gallon malted bran, 1 quart dried cracked corn, 1 quart oats and ¼ pound hops. Bring to a boil, then remove from heat and add 1½ gallons molasses. Let cool. When lukewarm, strain into a crock and add 3 cups homemade liquid yeast (or 3 yeast cakes dissolved in 3 cups warm water). Cover and let set overnight. Then bottle and cap.

39

**KEUMISS
(MILK BEER)** Combine 1 quart new milk, ½ cup fresh buttermilk and 4 teaspoons sugar. Mix until sugar dissolves, then cover and let stand in warm place until it is smooth and thick. Bottle, cork loosely and keep in a warm place 24 to 36 hours, depending on the temperature (the warmer the temperature, the less time needed). Then tighten the corks. Shake well before using.

**HONEY
ALE** Boil a handful of hops in 1 gallon of water for 20 minutes. Strain and cool to lukewarm, then add 1½ pounds honey and stir well. Pour into a clean crock. Cover and set in a warm, draft-free place to ferment. When bubbling activity stops (about 3 to 4 days) bottle and cap. Store in a cool place. May be used after 2 weeks.

**MODERN
BEER
(Easy Method)** Pour 10 gallons lukewarm water into 12-gallon stone crock. Dissolve ¼ cup brewers or homemade yeast or 1 pkg. or cake of yeast, one 3-lb. can hop-flavored malt syrup, 10 lbs. granulated sugar in the water and stir. Place covered with cheesecloth in warm place. Skim foam off top as required. Let work (3 to 5 days) until only about 10 needle bubbles per minute can be seen in center of liquid. Test with sacrometer (if available) should show 1 percent sugar content. Syphon into heavy glass quart bottles adding ¼ teaspoon of sugar to each bottle. Cap. Let age at least 10 days.

LAGER
BEER

1 pound dried malt extract
5 pounds granulated sugar
5 gallons boiling water
1 package beer yeast
¼ cup lukewarm water

Combine malt extract and sugar in a large crock or tub that will hold five gallons. Add boiling water and stir well to dissolve malt and sugar. Let set until lukewarm. Meanwhile, stir the beer yeast into ¼ cup lukewarm water and let set to dissolve. Test to be sure malt-sugar liquid is lukewarm, then add yeast liquid. Stir well. Pour into a 5-gallon glass or crockery jug.

Insert a 6-foot length of plastic tubing into the neck of the jug and seal it in the neck with putty, soft plastic or by drilling a hole in a cork. Set in a warm, draft-free place with the jug about three feet higher than the end of the tube. Keep the end of the tub immersed in a pan of water. Within 24 hours the beer should begin to ferment and air bubbles will escape through the tube. Keeping it under water will allow the bubbles to escape without allowing air (or insects) to enter the jug. The bubbling will continue for 3 to 4 days in warm weather and up to 6 to 8 days in colder weather.

When the bubbles slow to three bubbles per minute, it is time to bottle the brew. Be certain the fermentation has slowed to this point. If beer is bottled too late, it will be flat. If it is bottled too soon, the build-up of gases in the bottles may cause them to explode. Add ¼ teaspoon sugar to each bottle before filling, then siphon in the fermented beer, using the plastic tube through which the bubbles escaped. Keep the other end of the tube 3 to 4 inches above the bottom of the jug to avoid siphoning out any yeast sediment. The last few inches may be siphoned off and bottled separately at the end of bottling. Cap bottles firmly and set upright in a dark, cool place for 2 weeks to 2 years. The longer the storage, the better the flavor.

MAKING SOFT DRINKS

The forerunners of today's bottled soft drinks were cider and perry or cold water flavored with fruit juice or spices and a little bicarbonate of soda added for effervescence. Sometimes vinegar was added to give "bite" to shrubs and fruit vinegars.

The following recipes are very old. Many of them were used by Grandmother to make delicious, wholesome soft drinks for her family.

Your family will enjoy them, too.

EXTRACTING FRUIT JUICE

APPLES The best way to extract juice from apples is with a heavy fruit press, cider mill or lard press, using a variety of apples for best flavor. However, if you do not have such a press, you may try one of the following methods:

Without Heat:
Wash and core apples, without peeling. Chop fine, using coarse blade of food chopper. Mash with potato masher and strain juice through a jelly bag, squeezing to extract juice.

With Heat:

Wash and core apples without peeling. Slice or cut into small pieces. Cook in saucepan over low heat, adding only ½ cup water to 4 cups apples. Cover. When apples are well cooked and juicy, strain through a jelly bag.

APRICOTS Halve fruit without peeling. Remove seeds. Simmer over low heat in only enough water to keep from sticking. When soft and well cooked, put through a colander or potato ricer. Add small amount of water to juice and pulp.

BERRIES Wash and then crush the ripe strawberries, blueberries, blackberries, raspberries, elderberries, or loganberries. Heat to 180 degrees over low heat, stirring often to keep from sticking. Add ½ cup water to each 4 cups berries. When fruit is juicy, drain through a jelly bag.

CHERRIES Wash and pit tart or sweet cherries. Add ½ cup water to each quart of fruit. Mash with potato masher and heat to 180 degrees, stirring often. Drain in a cloth jelly bag.

GRAPES Grapes, like apples, are best crushed in a fruit or lard press. If you do not have a press, add ½ cup water to each quart of grapes and crush the fruit with a potato masher, then heat gradually to 180 degrees. Do not allow it to boil. Drain through a cloth bag and allow to stand overnight to let crystals form and settle. In the morning, carefully siphon off clear juice, discarding sediment and crystals.

GRAPEFRUIT Grapefruit may be cut in half without peeling and juiced with an orange juice extractor, or the fruit may be peeled and the pulp crushed in a fruit press or by hand. Do not heat and do not press with the rind on.

ORANGES Use directions for grapefruit.

PLUMS Wash and crush with potato masher, removing pits. Add 1 cup water to each quart of fruit. Cook over low heat until fruit is soft, being careful not to let pulp come to a boil or stick to the bottom. Drain in cloth bag.

RHUBARB Wash the smaller, most flavorful stalks and cut into 1-inch lengths. Add 1 cup water to each 2 quarts of rhubarb. Cover and heat over low heat. Cook without boiling until fruit is shredded and pulpy. Drain through cloth bag.

BOTTLING OR FREEZING FRUIT JUICES

To bottle high-acid fruit juices (all of the above plus to-mato juice), slowly heat extracted, strained juice to 190 degrees (use thermometer for best flavor), over indirect heat, as in a double boiler. Meanwhile, sterilize bottles by covering them with water and bringing the water to a boil, then simmering for 20 minutes over low heat.

Keeping the temperature of the juice at 190 degrees, fill the still-hot just-sterilized bottles, one at a time, with hot juice. Cap with cork-lined metal caps and invert bottles 5 minutes. Set in draft-free place to cool for 12 hours, then store upright in a dark, cool place.

Do *not* use this bottling method for low-acid vegetable juice, such as carrot or celery juice. Low-acid juices must be canned in a pressure canner, but the quality of product is not high. They are best used fresh or frozen.

Any juice — low-or high-acid — may be frozen in milk cartons or plastic containers for short term (3 to 4 months) freezer storage.

OTHER FRUIT DRINKS

RASPBERRY-CURRANT PUNCH

Mix 1 pint of raspberries and 1 quart of currants. Mash with a potato masher and add 2 quarts cold water. Heat gradually over low heat and bring just to a boil, then remove and strain through a jelly bag. Chill and serve, sweetened if you like.

TO PRESERVE APPLE CIDER

In order to keep apple cider for any length of time, it is necessary to clear it completely of any pomace (bits of apple) and store it in a place as near to freezing as possible. Bottled cider keeps better than that kept in a barrel.

OR:

Heat sweet cider slowly to the boiling point, then skim. Pour into sterilized bottles and cap immediately.

MULLED CIDER

Heat 1 quart of cider to boiling. Beat 2 eggs to very light color, adding ½ cup sugar. Pour the hot cider over the eggs. Stir and pour from one vessel to another until it foams. Serve hot.

OR:

Add 1 tablespoon whole cloves to 1 quart of cider and bring to a boil. Meanwhile beat 6 whole eggs in a large pitcher, adding ½ cup sugar as you beat. Pour the boiling hot cider on the beaten egg mixture, then back into the pot. Pour back and forth two or three times until frothy. Remove cloves and serve hot with a little grated nutmeg on top.

CIDER Cider is fruit juice, usually apple, which has been freshly pressed or allowed to ferment slightly. Cider can be made of grapes, cherries or almost any juicy, acid fruit. The first American homesteaders made delicious cider, which they called "perry," from the juice of crushed pears.

Cider is made by pressing the juice from the fruit, either in a cider press or by hand. Juice also may be extracted by chopping the fruit and using a tool such as a potato masher. The resulting juice then is strained through cheesecloth or coarse cloth. The best apple cider is made from a combination of tart, juicy apples, including crabapples.

The cider is kept in wooden kegs or glass jugs, stopped tightly. Nothing is added. It must be watched closely, however, for even when kept in a cold place, cider will quickly ferment to wine and will eventually turn to vinegar.

LEMON SYRUP Combine 3 pounds sugar and the grated rind of 6 lemons. Add 1 quart of water and stir over low heat until dissolved. Then cook until the syrup is thick, skimming off the scum as it rises. Remove from the fire and add the juice of the 6 lemons and mix well. Bottle and keep in a cool place.

To use add 1 part lemon syrup to 2 parts cold water.

STRAWBERRY SYRUP Crush very ripe strawberries and press the juice through cheesecloth or a jelly bag. To each pint of syrup add 1 cup sugar and 1 cup water. Simmer 20 minutes and cool. Bottle and keep cool. To use add water to taste and pour over crushed ice.

STRAWBERRY SODA

Simmer 1 quart strawberry juice over low heat until it boils down to 2 cups liquid. Add 1 pound sugar and stir to dissolve. Add 1½ ounces cream of tartar and cool. When cold, bottle and cap or cork tightly.

To use, fill an 8-ounce glass ¾ full of cold water and add 2 tablespoons of the syrup. Briskly stir in ½ teaspoon bicarbonate of soda.

RASPBERRY, CURRANT, GRAPE OR ORANGE SODA

Follow recipe above, substituting raspberry, currant, grape or orange juice for the strawberry juice.

SPICED DRINKS

GINGER POP

2 gallons water
2 pounds sugar
2 lemons
1 tablespoon cream of tartar
1 cup liquid homemade yeast (or 1 yeast cake
     dissolved in 1 cup warm water)
2 ounces dried ginger root, bruised

Boil the ginger root for 20 minutes in the water. Meanwhile grate the rind of the 2 lemons and squeeze the juice. Mix with the sugar and cream of tartar in a stone crock. Strain the ginger water into this and mix well. Cool to lukewarm, then add yeast. Stir well and cover. Let set in warm place for 24 hours, then bottle and cap. In 3 days it is ready to drink.

48

OR:

Boil ¼ pound bruised, dried ginger root for 30 minutes in 1 gallon of water. Strain off the water into a large crock and add 3 tablespoons lemon juice. Add 2½ pounds sugar, stir well, and add the stiffly-beaten whites of 3 eggs. Stir well and let cool to lukewarm by adding 4 more gallons of lukewarm water.

Stir in 2 cups liquid homemade yeast (or 2 yeast cakes dissolved in 2 cups warm water). Mix well and let set covered overnight in a warm, draft-free place. In the morning, bottle and cap. Store bottled in a cool place.

SPANISH GINGERETTE

To make 5 gallons, boil ½ ounce bruised, dried ginger and 2 sliced lemons in 2 gallons water for 20 minutes. Strain liquid into an 8-gallon crock and add 1 pound of sugar, ¼ ounce cream of tartar dissolved in ½ cup cold water and 3 gallons lukewarm water. Then add 1 cup liquid homemade yeast (or 1 yeast cake dissolved in 1 cup warm water) and mix well. Cover crock with a cloth and let set overnight. In the morning strain, bottle and cap. Store in a cool place.

SHAM CHAMPAGNE

Slice 1 large lemon and bruise 1 ounce dried ginger root. Mix with 1 ounce cream of tartar, 1½ pounds sugar and over all pour 2½ gallons boiling water. Let stand until lukewarm, then add 1 cup liquid homemade yeast (or 1 yeast cake dissolved in 1 cup warm water). Cover and let stand in the sun all day. When the sun goes down, bottle and cap. In two days it is ready to drink.

49

ARTIFICIAL CIDER

To 1 gallon cold water add 1 pound dark brown sugar, ½ ounce cream of tartar, 1 teaspoon of dry yeast (or 3 tablespoons liquid homemade yeast). Stir well and let stand overnight in warm place in a covered crock or keg. Bottle, putting 2 or 3 raisins in each bottle. Will keep 1 month in a cool place.

CREAM NECTAR

Dissolve 2 pounds sugar in 3 quarts of water. Boil down to 2 quarts and drop in the white of an egg while boiling. Strain and add 1 teaspoon cream of tartar. Cool. Add lemon juice to taste. Bottle and cap.

CREAM SODA

1 pound sugar
2 cups rich cream
1 quart water
1 tablespoon vanilla
¼ ounce cream of tartar

Combine ingredients and bring slowly to a boil over low heat. When it is just boiling, pour into a jar and cover. Keep in a cold place and use within a week.

To use, mix 1 tablespoon of the liquid and 1 teaspoon of bicarbonate of soda to 1 glass of ice water.

RASPBERRY VINEGAR

Mash 4 quarts fresh raspberries to a pulp, then add just enough cider vinegar to cover. Set close by a cookstove or over a hot water heater or heat register for 12 hours. Then strain and press through a jelly bag. Pour this juice over 4 more quarts of fresh raspberries. Cover and place in hot sun for 6 hours. Now strain, measure and add 1 pound of sugar for every pint of juice. Bring slowly to a boil over low heat. Strain, bottle and cap.

To use add 1 part to 3 or 4 parts cold water.

OR:

Pour 1 quart cider vinegar on 3 quarts ripe raspberries. Let stand 24 hours, then strain. Pour this liquid over 3 more quarts of fresh ripe berries and let infuse again for 24 hours. Strain again and add 1 pound of sugar to each pint of juice. Simmer over low heat 20 minutes, skimming well. Let cool, then bottle and seal. To use, add one part raspberry vinegar to 4 parts cold water.

OR:

Fill a stone crock with mashed, ripe raspberries and cover with cider vinegar. Let stand 5 days, then strain through a coarse cloth and to each pint of juice add 1 pound of sugar. Heat until sugar is dissolved. Skim, bottle and seal. For a summer drink stir 3 to 4 tablespoons into a glass of water.

LEMON VINEGAR

To 1 quart of cider vinegar add the rind of 2 or 3 lemons, peeled very thin. Cap the bottle and let stand 2 weeks. To use as a beverage, add 2 tablespoons to a glass of cold water. Sweeten to taste.

RASPBERRY SHRUB

For every cup of raspberry juice, add ½ cup white-wine vinegar and 2 cups sugar. Heat slowly until sugar dissolves, then boil to a thick syrup, stirring constantly. Bottle and keep in a cool place.

To use combine ¼ cup syrup to ¾ cup cold water.

HARVEST DRINK or SWITCHEL

Combine 1 cup of vinegar, 1 tablespoon molasses, 4 tablespoons sugar, 1½ quarts water and 1 teaspoon ground ginger. Mix well. Serve cold.

ROOT, BARK AND SPICE BEERS

Root beer has no alcoholic content. To make it, the flavor is extracted from roots and bark by boiling. Sugar and yeast then are added and the liquid is bottled immediately.

ROOT BEER
You'll need ½ ounce each of hops and dried burdock, yellow dock, sarsaparilla, dandelion, sassafras and spikenard roots for each gallon of water. Wash and bruise them well, using a potato masher or pie crust blender. Cover with the water and bring to a boil over high heat. Lower heat and simmer 20 minutes. While still hot strain into a large crock, discarding roots. Add 1½ cups molasses to each gallon of water and cool to lukewarm.

When lukewarm add 1 teaspoon dry yeast (or 2 tablespoons homemade liquid yeast) and stir well to mix.

53

Set the crock in a warm, draft-free corner where the temperature is 70 to 80 degrees. Cover with a cloth and let set two hours. Then bottle, filling to within ½ inch of the top. Cap bottles using capper and metal caps, not corks.

Place capped bottles on their sides in a warm (70 to 80 degree) draft-free place for 5 days, then set upright in a cool place. Root beer is ready to drink after 10 days, but will keep well through the summer.

BARK AND ROOT BEER

Gather a half bushel of mixed spruce boughs, sassafras roots, sarsaparilla roots, sweet fern, wintergreen leaves, black birch bark, black cherry bark, dandelion roots and burdock roots. Clean well, cut up and boil in 6 gallons of water to which has been added a large handful of hops and a quart of wheat bran. Cook 20 minutes, then strain through a sieve into a large crock. Add 3 quarts of molasses. Cool, then stir in 1 cup liquid yeast (or 1 yeast cake dissolved in 1 cup warm water). Cover and let set 3 days in a warm place. Bottle and cap. It will be ready to drink after 3 more days.

SPRUCE BEER

Into a large kettle put 10 gallons of water, ¼ pound of hops, 1 cup of dried, bruised ginger root and 2 pounds of the outer twigs of spruce fir. Boil together until all the hops sink to the bottom of the kettle, then strain into a large crock. Into this stir 6 quarts of molasses. Let cool and add 1 cup liquid homemade yeast or 1 yeast cake dissolved in a cup of warm water. Let set covered for 48 hours. Then bottle and cap. Let set 5 days in a warm place (70 to 75 degrees). Then it is ready to drink. Store upright in a cool place.

OR:

Boil a handful of hops and ½ pound of spruce twigs in 2½ gallons of water until the hops fall to the bottom of the kettle. Strain into a crock and add 1 tablespoon ground ginger and 1 pint molasses. Cool to lukewarm. Then add ½ cup liquid yeast or ½ yeast cake dissolved in ½ cup warm water. Mix well, then cover and let set 48 hours. Bottle and cap, putting 3 or 4 raisins in the bottom of each bottle.

GINGER BEER

Put 1½ pounds sugar, 3 ounces dried, bruised ginger root and the grated peel of 2 lemons in a large stone crock and pour 2 gallons boiling water over them. Cool to lukewarm, strain and put the liquid back into the crock. Add the juice of the 2 lemons and 2 tablespoons liquid yeast. Cover and let set overnight, then bottle and cap in the morning.

OR:

Boil 5 ounces bruised, dried ginger root in 3 quarts water 30 minutes. Strain into a large crock and add 5 pounds sugar, 1 cup lemon juice, ¼ pound honey and 4 gallons lukewarm water. Stir well, then add the white of 1 egg, beaten to a thick foam. Stir again. Cover and let stand in a warm (70 to 80 degrees) place 4 days. Bottle, using metal caps. Will keep several months. This recipe does not contain yeast but substitutes honey as an activator.

OR:

Boil ¾ ounce dried bruised ginger root in 1 gallon of water for 30 minutes. Add 1 pound sugar and 1 sliced lemon. Stir well, cool to lukewarm. Add 1 tablespoon liquid yeast or 1 teaspoon dry yeast dissolved in warm water. Let stand in a covered crock 24 hours, then strain and bottle, using caps. Will be ready to drink in 5 days.

SPICED GINGER BEER

To 2 ounces bruised, dried ginger root add 1 ounce ground allspice, ½ ounce ground cinnamon, ¼ ounce ground cloves and 8 gallons water. Boil 20 minutes, then strain into a small wooden keg and add 4 cups molasses and 2 tablespoons dissolved dry yeast or 1 cup liquid yeast. Shake well. Keep in a cool place until used. Do not fill keg more than three-fourths full.

PHILADELPHIA GINGER BEER

Boil ½ pound dried, bruised ginger root and 1 ounce of hops in 1 gallon of water for 30 minutes. Strain into a large crock and add 6 pounds brown sugar, 1 sliced lemon, 1 ounce bicarbonate of soda and 9 more gallons lukewarm water. Stir well. Then add 2 tablespoons dry yeast (or 1 cup liquid homemade yeast) and the beaten whites of 3 eggs. Cover and let stand in a warm place overnight. In the morning, skim, remove lemon slices and bottle with metal caps. Store upright in a cool place. Will keep several months.

CREAM GINGER BEER

Into a preserving kettle put 1½ ounces bruised, dried ginger root, 3 sliced lemons with rind, 1 handful hops and 2 quarts cold water. Bring to boil over low heat and let simmer 2 hours, then strain into large crock. Add 8 pounds sugar, 1 ounce cream of tartar, 10 quarts lukewarm water, 1 cup liquid yeast (or 1 yeast cake dissolved in 1 cup warm water) and the stiffly beaten whites of 6 eggs. Let set, covered, in a warm place 24 hours before bottling.

SUMMER BEER

Add 1 handful of hops to 2 quarts water and boil over low heat for 20 minutes. Strain into a crock and add 12 quarts lukewarm water, 1 quart molasses and 1 cup homemade yeast (or 1 yeast cake dissolved in 1 cup warm water.) Mix well and allow to settle. Strain through a coarse cloth and bottle with caps. Will be ready to drink in 24 hours.

CREAM BEER

Dissolve 2 ounces cream of tartar, 2 pounds sugar and the juice of 1 lemon in 3 pints of water. Heat to dissolve sugar, then cool. Add the stiffly beaten whites of 2 eggs mixed with ½ cup flour. Strain and bottle, adding 2 wintergreen leaves to each bottle. Cap and keep in a cool place. To use, add 2 tablespoons of the mixture to a glass of cold water, adding ¼ teaspoon bicarbonate of soda.

LEMON BEER

To 5 gallons water add 2 ounces bruised, dried ginger root and 1½ ounces cream of tartar. Simmer 30 minutes. Strain the hot liquid into a large crock and add 5 gallons lukewarm water. Add 4 pounds of sugar, 3 sliced lemons and 2 tablespoons dried yeast (or 1 cup homemade liquid yeast). Stir well. Cover with a cloth and set in a warm, draft-free place overnight.

The next day, skim the yeast on top, strain the liquid through 3 thicknesses of cheesecloth and bottle for use. Cap and keep in a cool place. It is best soon after making but will keep up to 3 weeks.